EDGE BOOKS™

SUPER TRIVIA COLLECTION

THIS BOOK IS HISTORY

BY CHRISTOPHER FOREST

A COLLECTION OF COOL U.S. HISTORY TRIVIA

Consultant:
Tim Solie
Adjunct Professor of History
Minnesota State University, Mankato

CAPSTONE PRESS
a capstone imprint

Edge Books are published by Capstone Press,
1710 Roe Crest Drive, North Mankato, Minnesota 56003.
www.capstonepub.com

Library of Congress Cataloging-in-Publication Data
Forest, Christopher.
    This book is history : a collection of cool U.S. history trivia / by Christopher Forest.
    p. cm.
    Includes bibliographical references and index.
    Summary: "Describes a variety of U.S. history trivia facts including the colonies,
Revolutionary War, Civil War, presidents, and monuments"—Provided by publisher.
    ISBN 978-1-4296-8419-4 (library binding)
    ISBN 978-1-62065-232-9 (ebook PDF)
    1. United States—History—Miscellanea—Juvenile literature. I. Title.
E178.3.F715 2013
973—dc23   2011048905

Editorial Credits
Aaron Sautter, editor; Tracy McCabe, designer; Wanda Winch, media specialist;
    Laura Manthe, production specialist

Photo Credits
Alamy: AAA Photostock, 8 (top), North Wind Picture Archives, 7 (t), 12 (bottom),
15 (b), 16 (all), 22; Bridgeman Art Library International/Virginia Historical Society,
Richmond Virginia, Alfred R. Waud, 26; Capstone, 9 (t), 17 (t), 27 (t), 28 (b); Corbis,
9 (b), Corbis: Royalty-Free, 10; Courtesy Gerald R. Ford Presidential Library, 24 (t);
Getty Images Inc: Stock Montage, 15 (t); iStockphotos: DHuss, 5 (b), miniature, 6
(left); Library of Congress: Prints and Photographs Division, 6 (right), 11 (b), 12 (t),
12 (middle), 13 (all), 14, 20, 21 (b), 23 (all), 25 (all), 28 (t), 29; National Archives and
Records Administration, 11 (t); Newscom: World History Archive, 19 (t); Shutterstock:
Andre Adams, 8 (b), AVprophoto, 17 (bl), Carsten Reisinger, 5 (t), Fernando Cortes,
graffiti design, FloridaStock, 19 (b), Guy J. Sagi, cover (br), HHsu, 21 (t), John T. Takai,
17 (br), JustASC, cover (t), marco mayer, 27 (b), Maximus256, 4-5 (U.S.map), Mike
Flippo, cover (bm), Piko72, 4 (l), Racheal Grazias, 18, Sergio Hayashi, 7 (b), Stephen
Finn, cover (bl), 1; Yesterday's Classics/The Baldwin Online Children's Literature
Project, www.mainlesson.com, 24 (b)

Printed in the United States of America in Stevens Point, Wisconsin.
032012   006678WZF12

TABLE OF CONTENTS

AMERICA'S LOST HISTORY

American history books are loaded with important dates, famous people, and exciting events. But textbooks don't tell the whole story. There are a lot of things about United States history that you may not know. For example, did you know that two U.S. presidents died on the exact same day? Do you know where the first shots of the Civil War (1861–1865) were really fired? Have you heard where the first settlement was in the United States? And you may not know it, but Uncle Sam was a real person!

Get ready to revise what you think you know. This book is filled with little-known facts about the states, people, and events that helped shape U.S. history. Soon you will be able to impress your friends with your newfound knowledge about America's history.

Chapter 1
UNUSUAL
LOCATION FACTS

Many locations across the United States have mysterious pasts. The history of these places has been overlooked or simply forgotten. Find out the truth about America's first **colony** and several other U.S. locations.

In 1784 several counties in western North Carolina decided to become the state of Franklin, named for Benjamin Franklin. However, the rest of  North Carolina's citizens didn't like the idea. They encouraged Congress to vote against the move. When it was time to vote, Congress said "no" to Franklin.

colony—a place that is settled by people from another country

Plymouth, Massachusetts, was not the original destination of the Pilgrims. They had hoped to settle along the Hudson River in New York. The land there was good for farming. But travel delays and the arrival of winter forced the Pilgrims to settle in Plymouth instead.

California is known for its oranges. However, oranges are not **native** to California. The first two orange trees were brought to California from Brazil in 1873. They were planted in Riverside, California. Most of the oldest California orange trees come from those two trees.

native—growing or living naturally in a particular place

St. Augustine, Florida

Jamestown, Virginia, was not the first colony in the United States. The first permanent European colony was actually St. Augustine, Florida. This Spanish colony was formed in 1565—42 years before Jamestown.

The United States has had three capitals since the U.S. Constitution was written in 1787. New York City served as the capital from 1789 to 1790. Then Philadelphia became the capital until 1800. Finally, in November of that year Washington, D.C., opened as the capital city.

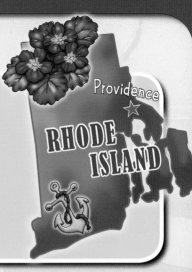

Rhode Island is the smallest state in total area. But it has the longest official name of any U.S. state. Its official name is "The State of Rhode Island and Providence Plantations."

In Europe during the 1700s, a lot of people had trouble paying their bills. These people were often arrested and put into **debtor's** prisons. But these prisons soon became overcrowded. In 1733 James Oglethorpe decided to solve the problem by creating the colony of Georgia in North America. Debtors were sent to Georgia to help reduce prison populations. Working in the new colony also gave debtors a chance to pay off their bills.

debtor—someone who owes money

Chapter 2
CONFOUNDING
COINCIDENCES

Sometimes events have strange connections to other events. These strange coincidences often happen when we least expect them. The following coincidences from U.S. history will make you stop and say, "No way!"

McLean home at Appomattox Court House, Virginia

In 1861 Wilmer McLean's home was located near Manassas, Virginia. The first major battle of the Civil War was the Battle of Bull Run, which took place on McLean's property. McLean later moved to the town of Appomattox Court House, Virginia. But he could not escape the war. In 1865 the Confederate Army surrendered to the Union—at McLean's house! After this event McLean supposedly said, "The war began in my front yard and ended in my front parlor."

John Adams and Thomas Jefferson had a lot in common. They both helped write the Declaration of Independence. They both served as U.S. president. And they both died on Independence Day in 1826—exactly 50 years after the Declaration of Independence was signed.

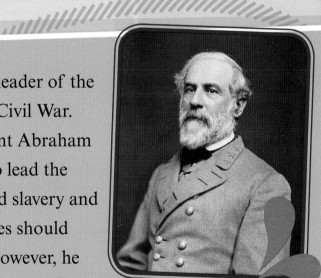

Robert E. Lee was the leader of the Confederate Army in the Civil War. But did you know President Abraham Lincoln once asked him to lead the Union Army? Lee opposed slavery and didn't think Southern states should **secede** from the Union. However, he was loyal to his home state of Virginia. He turned down Lincoln's offer, and chose to command Virginia's forces instead. Lee later became the general-in-chief of the Confederate Army.

secede—to formally withdraw from a group or organization

William McKinley

Rutherford B. Hayes

The 23rd regiment from Ohio fought bravely in the Civil War. Two future U.S. presidents served in the 23rd. One of the generals was Rutherford B. Hayes, who later became the 19th U.S. president. As an officer, Hayes twice promoted a soldier he considered courageous in battle. This soldier was William McKinley, who would go on to become America's 25th president.

The first lifelong slave in America was actually owned by a former **indentured servant**. In the 1600s these servants worked for a time in the American colonies and then were freed. Anthony Johnson was one such servant. He came from Africa, earned his freedom, and later owned a farm and servants of his own.

In 1640 he caught his servant John Casor trying to run away. He took Casor to court, which later ruled that Casor was Johnson's "servant for life."

indentured servant—a type of slave who works for another person in exchange for travel or living costs

Samuel Adams was one of the most important leaders of the Revolutionary War (1775–1783). He led the Boston Sons of Liberty in their fight for freedom. And he often made speeches to protest British taxation. But his earlier job might surprise you. From 1756 to 1764 he worked as a British tax collector in Massachusetts.

Robert Todd Lincoln

You may know that John Wilkes Booth **assassinated** Abraham Lincoln. But did you know that Booth's brother Edwin once saved a Lincoln? One day in 1864, Edwin was waiting at a train station in Jersey City, New Jersey. When he saw a young man fall into the space between a train and the platform, he rushed into action. Edwin grabbed the young man by the collar and pulled him up, just as the train began to move. The man Edwin rescued was none other than Robert Todd Lincoln—Abraham's son!

assassinate—to murder a person who is well known or important

Chapter 3
AMAZING
EVENTS

The Revolutionary War, the Lewis and Clark **expedition**, and the Civil War all changed the course of U.S. history. However, these events and others included episodes that might surprise you.

Most Americans believe the United States declared its independence from Great Britain on July 4, 1776. But that isn't quite true. The **Continental Congress** actually voted to declare independence on July 2. But Congress did not officially approve the final text of the Declaration of Independence until July 4.

expedition—a journey with a specific goal, such as exploring or searching for something

Continental Congress—leaders from the 13 original American colonies

James Madison's wife, Dolley, saved a big part of U.S. history during the War of 1812 (1812–1815). In 1814 the British attempted to burn down the White House. Before she fled the burning building, Dolley saved several important papers. These documents included the Declaration of Independence and the first draft of the U.S. Constitution.

In 1587 Governor John White left the English colony on Roanoke Island in North Carolina to bring back supplies from England. But a war between England and Spain prevented him from returning until 1590. When he returned, the people of Roanoke had disappeared. The mystery was never solved. Roanoke eventually became known as "The Lost Colony." Historians believe that American Indians or nearby Spanish settlers may have attacked the colony. Others think the colonists simply joined one of the local American Indian tribes.

Robert L. Livingston is often a forgotten patriot. He helped write the Declaration of Independence, but he never put his name on it. He had to return to his job in New York before he could sign it.

One of the most important battles in the Revolutionary War was the Battle of Bunker Hill in 1775. However, the battle did not actually take place on Bunker Hill. The colonists had planned to take control of Bunker Hill. But as they made their move during the night, they accidentally took over nearby Breed's Hill instead. Some historians believe that a map error led to the Americans taking the wrong hill.

Sacagawea is famous for helping Meriwether Lewis and William Clark on their expedition to the West. But no one really knows if Sacagawea was her real name. Sacagawea was a Shoshone Indian. As a child she had been kidnapped and forced to live with the Hidatsa tribe. She may have taken a new name with the Hidatsa.

The 1849 Gold Rush in California was not the first time gold was discovered in the United States. When gold was discovered in Dahlonega, Georgia, it sparked a gold rush about 21 years earlier.

Georgia

Chapter 4
MONUMENTAL MARVELS

Major monuments like Mount Rushmore and the Statue of Liberty symbolize American freedoms. However, there is more to these symbols than meets the eye. Secrets and mysteries surround several U.S. monuments that few people have ever heard about.

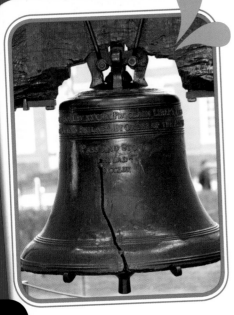

The famous Liberty Bell in Philadelphia, Pennsylvania, has an outdated spelling. Pennsylvania is actually spelled *Pensylvania* on the bell. In 1753 there was no official way to spell Pennsylvania. The Liberty Bell spelling was acceptable at the time. The U.S. Constitution contains the same outdated spelling.

The Statue of Liberty has gone through a lot of changes since it was first dedicated in 1886. First, its official name, "Liberty Enlightening the World," has almost been forgotten. The statue's original torch was replaced in 1986. And the color of the statue has changed over time. The statue is made of copper and originally had a shiny red-brown color. A chemical change called patination has given the copper statue its current greenish color.

The bald eagle became the symbol of the United States in 1782. It was chosen for its strength, beauty, and majesty. However, bald eagles nearly lost out to turkeys! Benjamin Franklin wanted to make the turkey the national bird. He thought turkeys were smart and crafty. He felt that eagles were cowardly and unfit to symbolize America.

"Plymouth Rock" In Front of Pilgrim Hall "1834"
Copyright A.W. Anderson

1620

Some history books say that the Pilgrims landed at Plymouth Rock in Massachusetts. But the Pilgrims never mention the rock in their writings. In 1741 a man named Elder Faunce declared the rock to be the Pilgrim stepping-stone. Faunce claimed that his father knew several Pilgrims who had told him about the rock. Faunce's story was told and retold for many years. In 1774 the residents of Plymouth placed the rock in front of the town's meetinghouse. An iron fence was later built around the rock to help keep it safe. The story of Plymouth Rock has been part of the Pilgrim story ever since.

The Gateway Arch in St. Louis, Missouri, symbolizes the city's status as the "Gateway to the West." During the 1800s St. Louis was the last stop before many settlers headed west. The city also served as a base camp for the famous Lewis and Clark expedition. At 630 feet (192 meters) tall, the Gateway Arch is the tallest man-made monument in the United States. It is taller than both the Washington Monument and the Statue of Liberty.

Mount Rushmore was originally designed to have a secret vault behind the presidential heads. Designer Gutzon Borglum wanted the vault to be a Hall of Records for copies of important U.S. documents. Borglum died before the hall could be completed. However his dream lived on. In 1998 the U.S. government finished the hall. Copies of the Declaration of Independence, the U.S. Constitution, and the Bill of Rights were sealed inside a vault that is meant to last for thousands of years.

Chapter 5

PECULIAR
PRESIDENTS

U.S. presidents hold many important roles like chief executive and commander in chief of the armed forces. However, like all people, presidents' lives often include unusual events.

U.S. President James Madison took his role of commander in chief of the military seriously. During the War of 1812, Madison tried to take command on the battlefield when the British army invaded Washington, D.C. However, he proved ineffective and had to retreat with the soldiers. Madison became the first and only U.S. president to face enemy fire in battle while holding the office.

William Henry Harrison served the shortest time of any U.S. president. The country's ninth president served for just 31 days. On March 4, 1841, he became sick on his first day as president. His cold later turned to pneumonia, which caused his death.

President Harry S. Truman had no middle name. His parents could not decide which of his grandfathers, Solomon Young or Anderson Shippe, to use for his middle name. Rather than picking one name, Harry's parents settled on a simple "S" instead.

Martin Van Buren was the eighth president of the United States. He was also the first president to be a natural-born citizen of the United States. The previous seven presidents were born in America, but it was part of Britain at the time. Van Buren was born December 5, 1782—more than six years after the Declaration of Independence was signed.

Gerald Ford

Talk about luck. Gerald Ford was the only person to serve as both vice president and president and never be voted into either office. In 1973 Ford was serving as the Speaker of the House in the U.S. House of Representatives. When Vice President Spiro Agnew was forced to resign, Ford was chosen to replace him. Then Ford became president when Richard Nixon resigned in 1974.

As a young man, President Abraham Lincoln had an interesting pastime—he was a wrestler! In 1831 Lincoln was living in New Salem, Illinois. A group of rowdy men known as the Clary's Grove Boys liked to challenge people to wrestling matches. One day a local grocer said that his clerk could beat their best wrestler. The groups' leader, Jack Armstrong, took up the challenge. "Honest Abe" soundly defeated Armstrong in one of several matches he fought in town.

Abraham Lincoln (left)

John Tyler is the only U.S. president to eventually turn against his own country. In 1841 John Tyler was elected as vice president. When president William Henry Harrison died, Tyler became president until 1845. But when the Civil War broke out, Tyler joined the Confederacy.

John Tyler

The longest serving president was Franklin D. Roosevelt. He was elected to the office four times. He led the United States during the **Great Depression** in the 1930s and at the beginning of World War II (1939–1945). Roosevelt died on April 12, 1945, shortly after starting his fourth term. He served 4,422 days in office. Later a constitutional amendment limited presidents to serving two four-year terms in office.

Great Depression—a period of hard economic times in the United States from 1929 to 1939

Chapter 6

INCREDIBLE INCIDENTS

U.S. history is filled with many famous stories. However, sometimes the stories didn't happen quite the way you might remember. Take a look at the truth behind some of these historical events.

Most history books say the Civil War started with the battle at Fort Sumter in South Carolina on April 12, 1861. But the first shots were actually fired three months earlier. On January 9, 1861, southern soldiers on Morris Island, South Carolina, opened fire on the Union steamship *Star of the West*. The ship was taking supplies to Fort Sumter.

Paul Revere was not the only person who made the famous midnight ride on April 18, 1775. William Dawes and Samuel Prescott also rode out to warn people that British soldiers were coming. Why do we remember Revere and not the others? Revere was made famous by a poem written by Henry Wadsworth Longfellow.

The first Thanksgiving may not have been celebrated by the Pilgrims. On September 8, 1565, explorer Pedro Menedez de Aviles celebrated a thanksgiving feast in what is now St. Augustine, Florida. He dined with the local Timucua Indians. And turkey wasn't the main food for the day. They ate bean soup instead!

John Hanson

If you thought the first U.S. president was George Washington, you'd be wrong. George Washington did serve as the first president elected under the U.S. Constitution. However, from 1777 to 1789, the country had an earlier constitution called the Articles of Confederation. The Continental Congress was responsible at this time for electing presidents to lead the country. The first president to serve under the full Articles of Confederation was John Hanson.

According to legend, no Americans survived the Battle of the Alamo in 1836. But some historians think a few defenders of the Alamo may have survived the fight, including Davy Crockett. However, after the battle the Mexican army supposedly **executed** them.

execute—to put to death

I WANT YOU
FOR U.S. ARMY
NEAREST RECRUITING STATION

Uncle Sam isn't just a cartoon character seen in posters. He was actually a real person. Samuel Wilson had a meat-packing business in New York. In the 1800s he supplied meat to soldiers in the army. His company put the initials "U.S." on its packages. During the War of 1812, soldiers began referring to "U.S." as "Uncle Sam" Wilson. Soon Uncle Sam became as American as apple pie. The cartoon image we know today as Uncle Sam was first drawn by Thomas Nast in 1869.

HUNTING FOR HISTORY TRIVIA

As you can see, a lot of little-known facts about U.S. history are just waiting to be found. Keep researching the important people and events that have shaped U.S. history. You may find something interesting that will surprise your family and friends!

GLOSSARY

assassinate (us-SASS-uh-nate)—to murder a person who is well known or important

colony (KAH-luh-nee)—a place that is settled by people from another country and is controlled by that country

Continental Congress (kahn-tuh-NEN-tuhl KAHN-gruhs)—leaders from the 13 original American colonies who made up the American government from 1774 to 1789

debtor (DET-tuhr)—someone who owes money to another person or organization

execute (EK-si-kyoot)—to put to death

expedition (ek-spuh-DI-shuhn)—a journey with a specific goal, such as exploring or searching for something

Great Depression (GRAYT di-PRESH-uhn)—a period of hard times from 1929 to 1939 in the United States when many people lost their jobs and had little money or food

indentured servant (in-DEN-churd SERV-uhnt)—a type of slave who works for someone else for a period of time in return for payment of travel and living costs

native (NEY-tiv)—growing or living naturally in a particular place

secede (si-SEED)—to formally withdraw from a group or organization, often to form another organization

READ MORE

Klutz, ed. *The Slightly Odd History of the United States.* Palo Alto, Calif.: Klutz, 2010.

Marsh, Carole. *Civil War Trivia: True Facts, Tall Tales, Fascinating Folklore, Stories, Songs, Journals, and More!* Peachtree City, Ga.: Gallopade Int., 2010.

Price, Sean. *U.S. Presidents: Truth and Rumors.* Truth and Rumors. Mankato, Minn.: Capstone Press, 2010.

INTERNET SITES

FactHound offers a safe, fun way to find Internet sites related to this book. All of the sites on FactHound have been researched by our staff.

Here's all you do:

Visit *www.facthound.com*

Type in this code: 9781429684194

Check out projects, games and lots more at
www.capstonekids.com

INDEX

59257